JOHN THE BAPTIST

AND PRAYERS OF SAINT

About Wyatt North Publishing

Starting out with just one writer, Wyatt North Publishing has expanded to include writers from across the country. Our writers include college professors, religious theologians, and historians.

Wyatt North Publishing provides high quality, perfectly formatted, original books.

Send us an email and we will personally respond within 24 hours! As a boutique publishing company we put our readers first and never respond with canned or automated emails. Send us an email at hello@WyattNorth.com, and you can visit us at www.WyattNorth.com.

Foreword

In understanding true poverty, practicing total detachment, lacking pride and demonstrating only obedience, John epitomized the call of Jesus Christ for his followers to take up their cross and follow him, before the true meaning of his words were even understood.

While Jesus himself described John the Baptist as a burning and shining lamp, John understood he was born only to direct us to the light of the Savoir.

Expressing heartfelt gratitude for the sacrifice, suffering and dedication to God shown by John the Baptist, all Christians today can bask in the light of Jesus.

Table of Contents

Quick Facts

The new "Quick Facts" section in **The Life and Prayers** collection provides the reader with a collection of facts about each saint!

Born:

5 BC, Jerusalem

Died:

28 AD, Machaerus

Feast:

June 24 (Nativity),
August 29 (Beheading),
January 7 (Synaxis,
Eastern Orthodox),
Thout 2 (Coptic Orthodox Church)

Attributes:

Camel-skin robe, cross, lamb

The Life of Saint John the Baptist

Born For A Purpose

*A*men, I say to you, among those born of women there has been none greater than John the Baptist; (Matthew 11:11)

St John the Baptist has beguiled and inspired Christians through the ages. An enigmatic figure, he is perhaps most familiar to Christians and non-Christians alike as a hermit wandering through the desert, clad in a camel hair tunic and a leather belt, surviving only on wild honey and locusts. To many he is also renowned as the proclaimer and baptizer of Jesus Christ.

Whatever he represents, one thing is certain; the unshakeable faith of John the Baptist continues to inspire Christians today. Beneath the surface of this iconic figure, lies the story of a selfless man; a man of unprecedented humility who unquestioningly surrendered his life to God's will; a man filled with the Holy Spirit even before he was born.

History has presented John the Baptist in several lights. Some scholars see him purely as a son of Second Temple Judaism, born of a Levite priest, yet his presence in a temple or in Jerusalem itself was never recorded. Others link him with the ancient nomadic Essene tribe, but during his time in the desert John the Baptist adopted the life of an ascetic hermit, seeking only intimacy with God in his solitude.

His contemporaries were both fascinated by him and wary of him, sometimes in equal amounts. With his passionate unyielding approach to preaching, some at first mistook him for their longed for Messiah. During his ministry he didn't perform a single miracle yet was referred to as Elijah in spirit by Jesus Christ himself.

While we may find contradicting portrayals and opinions of John the Baptist amongst Christian scholars, for many he was without question the first saint and Christian martyr before the Christian faith had been established.

The evidence for the life of this revered saint is found within the Gospels, the Book of Acts and in Jewish historian Flavius Josephus' *Antiquities of the Jews*, which is believed to have been written around AD

93. Moreover, John the Baptist is unique because he is featured in all four gospels, where he is presented as prophet, preacher, forerunner, witness to and disciple of Jesus Christ.

The ministry of this fiery preacher may have only lasted two years but, with the exception of Lord Jesus Christ and the Virgin Mary, his is the only feast day, which is celebrated on the date of his birth, and he is the only man believed to have been born without original sin.

John the Baptist was born for a purpose; that purpose was to fulfill the Old Testament prophecies, to prepare for the arrival of the long awaited Messiah; to minister in the spirit and power of the revered prophet Elijah and to return God's people back to him. Throughout his life he fulfilled that purpose, offering utter and unquestioning obedience to God's will.

As the words of Jesus Christ himself at the opening of this chapter show us, there has been no man born greater than St John the Baptist, a greatness which began before he was born.

Fulfillment of the Prophecies

The ministry of John the Baptist was prophesied over four centuries before his birth and reference to him can be found in the Old Testament books of Isaiah and Malachi.

Perhaps the most well know prophecy is that of Isaiah:-

''A voice proclaims: In the wilderness prepare the way of the Lord! Make straight in the wasteland a pathway for our God!' (Isaiah 40:3)

His words are reiterated by Malachi who refers to a messenger who will *'pave the way before me' (Malachi 3:1)*. Malachi also speaks of the return of the prophet Elijah. To put the prophecies into context, at the time of the birth of John the Baptist in approximately 4 AD, four and a half centuries had elapsed since the time of Malachi, the last prophet of Israel. God had kept the Israeli people waiting for a considerable time but their patience was soon to be rewarded.

John the Baptist was born Yochanan Ben Zechariah to his mother Elizabeth, a reputed cousin of Mary, and father Zechariah, an Aaronic priest in the order of Abijah, established by King David. Both parents were devout and God fearing people who had longed for a child of their own.

In the opening of Luke's gospel, the angel Gabriel appears to Zechariah to foretell of the birth of his son:-

'But the angel said to him, "Do not be afraid, Zechariah, because your prayer has been heard. Your wife Elizabeth will bear you a son, and you shall name him John. And you will have joy and gladness, and many will rejoice at his birth, for he will be great in the sight of [the] Lord. He will drink neither wine nor strong drink. He will be filled with the Holy Spirit even from his mother's womb and he will turn many of the children of Israel to the Lord their God. He will go before him in the spirit and power of Elijah to turn the hearts of fathers towards children and the disobedient to the understanding of the righteous, to prepare a people fit for the Lord' (Luke 1:13-17.

Gabriel's words clearly show that John the Baptist is to fulfill the prophecies of both Isaiah and Malachi.

The miraculous blessing of God on a childless couple has a Biblical precedence in the story of Abraham and Sarah in the book of Genesis, which was likely familiar to John's parents. It is estimated that Zechariah and Elizabeth were in their thirties or forties at the time of John's birth. At the time, most babies were born to young women in their teens.

The fulfillment of the angel Gabriel's prophecies are seen almost immediately as Mary, pregnant with the son of God, visited Elizabeth to tell her of her own good news. Full of the Holy Spirit before he is born, John *'leaped for joy'* in his mother's womb as he recognized the presence of Jesus. *(Luke 1:41)*. Already the unborn John the Baptist was obeying God's call on his life.

John's predestined role was immediately becoming clear. An incredulous Zechariah, however, had originally doubted the word of the angel. As a consequence, he was struck dumb until after the circumcision of his son, where he obeyed God's instructions given to him by the Angel Gabriel and named his son John.

Luke's opening chapter also contains The Canticle of Zechariah, which he recited on being blessed with the return of his speech. Zechariah's canticle praised God and prophesized that John will be called a *'prophet of the Most High' (Luke 1:76),* emphasizing his primary role as going *'before the Lord'* to prepare his people.

It is not certain as to whether John's father, Zechariah and his mother Elizabeth bore further children. What is certain is that John the Baptist was a man of God, a fulfilment of the prophecies of both Isaiah and Malachi centuries before he was born.

The Wilderness of John the Baptist

Much of the events of John the Baptist's life invite parallels with the life of Jesus. As the forerunner of Jesus Christ, John is a type of mirror image. Rather than reflect the greatness of Jesus, he deflects the attention of the people towards the Messiah. This is perhaps inevitable to enable him to pave the way for the Messiah.

Like Jesus, details of John's life from his birth until his ministry are sparse. After announcing John's birth, the only available detail of is life is the reference in Luke's gospel to him growing and becoming *'strong in spirit'*. From that point onwards, he remained in the desert until the *'day of his manifestation to Israel'* (*Luke 1:80*). It is believed that at the time John entered the desert to begin his penance, his parents, Zechariah and Elizabeth, were no longer alive as they are not mentioned again in the Scriptures.

As a Jewish boy and the son of a priest, John would have received his bar mitzvah at the age of twelve and would have had the option of becoming a priest himself. Scholars believe that it was probably from this age until he began his ministry at the estimated age of thirty that John began his years of wilderness in the desert of Judea to prepare for his role commissioned by God – that of the precursor to Jesus Christ.

Historian Origen, a third century theologian, summarizes the reason for John's sojourn in the desert in his Homily 11:-

'He did so in order to spend his time in prayer in the company of the angels for the time of baptizing and preaching had not yet arrived'

According to Jewish and Near Eastern traditions of the time, the desert was seen as sacred ground and the dwelling place of God. In the Old Testament, this tradition is perhaps most familiar in the story of Moses' encounter with God at the burning bush on the isolated plains of Mount Horeb; a story found in the book of Exodus. Moses subsequently led his people into the desert where they endured forty years in the wilderness as they waited to cross into the Promised Land.

The prophet Elijah, whose spirit John the Baptist was said to represent, also spent a brief time in the wilderness of the desert. When prophesying against the Baal people, Elijah fled to the desert to escape persecution. *(1 Kings 19)*.

If the presence of the Holy Spirit within John the Baptist was to be the fundamental influence in his life, as prophesied by Gabriel, then two decades spent in the desolate landscape of the Judean desert would allow its full manifestation. Luke's earlier reference to John becoming strong in spirit reveals a fortitude and strength that would be necessary to equip him for his future ministry among the Jewish people.

The desert was not without its spiritual dangers, however. Within Jewish culture, it possessed two distinctly opposite traits. While it was seen as providing an environment of solitude for intimate encounters with God, its remoteness was also believed to be an ideal habitat for Satan and evil spirits. Trials and suffering would have been inevitable. The temptation of Christ himself took place in the desolation of the desert so it is unlikely that John the Baptist would have been immune.

The ascetic life adopted by John the Baptist would require obedience to God in the face of extreme struggles and temptation. Indeed, the extent of his deprivation and trials endured in the abandoned landscape of the Judean desert can only be guessed. Guided by the Holy Spirit, John's life became one of prayer, fasting and solitude as he sought God's presence and surrendered to His will. Luke's gospel makes it clear that the word of God came to him in the desert. *(Luke 3:2)*.

Unlike Elijah who was fed by the ravens *(1 Kings 17:6)* and later an angel, it seems John the Baptist was left to fend for himself. With scorching summer temperatures, food may not have been easy to come by, resulting in a meager diet of locusts and wild honey *(Matt 3:4)*.

Often in art, John is depicted as an emaciated hermit, the result of a detached and ascetic lifestyle. His detachment from his family, society and even his own will could only have been learned in the desert terrain. This rare detachment extended into his ministry as he is recorded as neither eating bread nor drinking wine *(Luke 7:33)* as prophesied by the Angel Gabriel before his birth.

John the Baptist is unique among men in surrendering to God's calling on his life in one of the most desolate places on Earth.

Epistle 125 from <u>Letters of St Jerome</u> reflects on this unique devotion to both God's call and Christ himself:-

'John the Baptist had a saintly mother and his father was a priest but neither his mother's love nor his father's wealth could prevail upon him to live in his parents' house at the risk of his chastity. He took up his abode in the desert and desiring only to see Christ refused to look at anything else'.

When his time for baptizing and preaching finally arrived, the impact of John the Baptist was revolutionary.

The Ministry of John the Baptist

After living the austere life of a hermit for perhaps two decades, dedicated to self-denial, prayer and fasting, this enigmatic holy man finally appeared to begin his public ministry.

The desert ministry of John the Baptist is believed to have taken place within forty miles of his home, amid the hilly terrain of west Jerusalem. It is hard to envisage the impact of this gaunt recluse as he emerged to pave the way for the Lord Jesus, preaching repentance and the dawn of a new era. Matthew's gospel describes crowds of people from Jerusalem and the whole of the Judean countryside flocking to hear his words (*Matt 3:5*), perhaps travelling on foot from up to eighty miles away.

The immediacy of his impact on the Jewish people is perhaps unsurprising. As we have seen, Israel had lacked a prophet for four and a half centuries and the political climate of the time would have contributed towards the peoples' eagerness to hear the words of their new prophet.

At the time of the ministry of John the Baptist, the Israeli people were also subject to the whim of unscrupulous rulers. Roman Emperor Tiberius had reigned for fifteen years, while the ruthless figure of Pontius Pilate governed Judea. Furthermore, Herod of Antipas, who was to be the direct target of John the Baptist's wrath for his marriage to his brother's wife, ruled Galilee. Corruption and greed dominated the political landscape, leaving a people yearning for the arrival of the promised Messiah, the new spirit of Elijah.

As he called out in the desert, it was becoming apparent that John the Baptist had come to fulfil the prophecies of the Old Testament, the Angel Gabriel and of his father Zechariah; to urge the Jewish people to turn away from sin and 'make the paths straight' for Jesus.

This stark, cadaverous man, who had conversed with no-one except God in the previous two decades, greeted the throngs of Israelites with uncompromising apocalyptic prophecies and warnings of repentance, revealing his true purpose in the first words that he uttered:-

'Repent for the Kingdom of Heaven is at hand' (Matt 3:2).

Indeed, it was here that John the Baptist begins his public ministry, preaching *'a baptism of repentance for the forgiveness of sins' (Mark 1:4)* and carrying out the baptisms in the River Jordan itself. It was here too, as he began his public ministry, amid patiently waiting crowds, that John became the gateway for the gospels themselves. As he greeted the crowds on the banks of the river, John the Baptist began to point the way to the ultimate fulfilment of all of the laws and the prophets, the coming of Jesus Christ.

The baptism of repentance carried out by John marked a subtle shift in the traditional baptism rituals carried out by the Jewish people of the time. Clearly laid out instructions in the book of Leviticus directed the Israeli people to regularly cleanse themselves through daily rituals to achieve purification of the body. At a time when contagious diseases such as leprosy were rife, this was not seen as unusual. Moreover, it allowed the Jewish people to carry out their ritual temple sacrifices, knowing they were fully cleansed.

In contrast, John's baptisms occurred once only with no associated requirement for temple sacrifices. Through his baptism, John gave the people the opportunity to seek forgiveness for their sins and commit to a new way of life. During his ministry and preaching, John did not once make reference to the temple.

The spirit filled John the Baptist intuitively understood that repentance was the first step towards spiritual growth and the forgiveness of sins. Today, this principle remains fundamental to the sacrament of reconciliation throughout the Catholic faith.

The emphasis of John's baptism is that of purification through water, implying preparation for a baptism by the Holy Spirit or Holy Spirit and fire *(Mark 1:8, Matt 3:11, Luke 3:16)* by Jesus himself. With their public nature, John's baptisms also represented a move away from the old traditions of private baptisms, which could be self-administered.

Moreover – and in contrast to the insular Jewish rituals - the baptisms performed by John were offered to all of the people, regardless of social standing. The words of Jesus in Matthew's gospel reveal tax collectors and prostitutes mingling in the teeming crowds on the banks of the River Jordan:-

'When John came to you in the way of righteousness, you did not believe him; but tax collectors and prostitutes did.' (Matt 21:32)

Furthermore, Luke records both tax collectors and soldiers seeking John's advice on how they might become righteous in the eyes of God *(Luke 3:12-14).*

To the people, John the Baptist was a radical. What's more, the extent of his radical nature was underlined by the fact that a man, who could have chosen to become a Levite priest, like his father before him, both rejected the religious authorities and ignored the temple in his baptisms. Again, the impact of his actions on the Jewish people cannot be underestimated.

Who was this hermit who emerged from the desert without warning and began baptizing people on the banks of the River Jordan – and not simply the elite but society's rejects, numbering prostitutes and tax collectors among them?

Who was he indeed.

In yet another radical departure from traditional Jewish belief, John also proclaimed that the descendants of Abraham could not guarantee their salvation purely through claiming the great patriarch as their father:-

And do not presume to say to yourselves, 'We have Abraham as our father.' For I tell you, God can raise up children to Abraham from these stones'. (Matt 3:9).

For John, the emphasis was firmly on repentance to avoid the coming wrath and judgment of God, yet just as the Jewish people could not rely on Abraham for their salvation, nor could they simply repent and continue their life as before. Words alone were inadequate; John believed that living a life of good works was vitally important to demonstrate repentance and escape damnation.

As Josephus explains in his <u>Antiquities of the Jews</u>:-

'They must not employ it to gain pardon for whatever sins they committed, but as a consecration of the body implying that the soul was already thoroughly cleansed by right behavior'.

The extent of the imminent upheaval of the old order was rapidly becoming apparent, reinforced by John's eschatological preaching, which was laden with images of judgment and fire. Eschatology is concerned with 'end times', a concept with which the Jewish people would have been all too familiar.

In addition, in a challenge to the religious order of the time, he refers to the Jewish religious authorities, the Pharisees and Sadducees, as *'a brood of vipers'* while warning of the coming Messiah separating the wheat from the chaff on judgment day:-

'He will clear his threshing floor and gather his wheat into his barn, but the chaff he will burn with unquenchable fire (Matt 3:12)

John's sole intention was to fulfil his God given purpose prophesied by the Angel Gabriel, to return the people of Israel back to God, and, in doing so, become the *'prophet of the 'Most High'* as foreseen by his father Zechariah.

Yet what of the prophecy of John the Baptist being the spirit of Elijah, testified to by the Angel Gabriel? Certainly, there were several similarities between these two holy men. Both wore similar clothing, camel hair tunics and leather belts. As we have seen, Elijah was exiled in the desert, albeit briefly and forced to consume scraps of meat delivered to him by ravens, while John foraged for locusts and wild honey.

Elijah performed many miracles through the work of the Holy Spirit while the Word of God came to John through the Holy Spirit. Like Elijah, John the Baptist was a prophet and priest, descended from the house of Levi in the order of Abijah, with a mission to reconcile the people back to God to prepare for the way for the coming of the Messiah. Similarly, Elijah's own mission of reconciliation is emphasized by both Malachi and Sirach.

On the other hand, Elijah did not preach on the coming of the Messiah, whereas for John the Baptist, this was one of the principal purposes of his ministry. Elijah performed miracles while John did not, yet he was filled with the Holy Spirit and spoke the word of God to such an extent that at times he was mistakenly believed to be the Messiah.

For all of the differences and similarities, it is the words of Jesus Christ himself that confirm the spirit of Elijah in the ministry of John the Baptist after his Transfiguration on the mountain that saw the appearance of both Elijah and Moses:-

'Elijah has already come, and they did not recognize him but did to him whatever they pleased. So also will the Son of Man suffer at their hands' (Matt 17:12)

With his austere appearance and ascetic life of self-denial and submissiveness to God's will, combined with his fiery preaching, it is unsurprising that the people believed at first that John the Baptist was indeed the Messiah himself, such was the level of hope and expectancy in their hearts.

Yet for a man like John the Baptist who devoted his life to chastity, poverty and obedience to God's will, his only desire was to prepare God's people for the one who was to come after *'whose sandal strap I am not worthy to untie'. (John 1:27)*

Baptizer and Witness

T

he focal point of John the Baptist's ministry was of course his baptism of the Lord Jesus in the River Jordan, an event which epitomizes his role as the forerunner of Christ, providing the gateway for the gospels and the dawn of the much heralded new era.

The event was significant. Firstly, John's baptism of Jesus represents the sole occasion that the adult John encounters the Messiah face to face and the second time that he recognizes his presence – the previous occasion being the response of the unborn child leaping in his mother's womb in the opening of Luke's gospel.

Secondly, such is the importance of Jesus' baptism, it is mentioned in all four of the gospels, although the apostle John refers to it more obliquely than the writers of the synoptic gospels. Indeed, it is only in the synoptic gospels and in Josephus' Antiquities of the Jews that John is referred to by the name of John the Baptist. John the evangelist describes John the Baptist only as a witness to Christ in his fourth gospel. As we will see, however, he did not deny his significance in the paving the way for Jesus.

Where John normally baptized people for repentance of their sins, this was of course needless in the sake of Jesus. Initially, John expressed an understandable reluctance to baptizing Jesus, believing that it was John himself who should be baptized. In all of the Synoptic gospels, Jesus is anointed with the Holy Spirit represented in the shape of a dove and the voice of God is heard as the heavens open above him:-.

'On coming up out of the water he saw the heavens being torn open and the Spirit, like a dove, descending upon him. And a voice came from the heavens, "You are my beloved Son; with you I am well pleased' (Mark 1:10-11)

While John the Apostle and writer of the fourth gospel does not record the actual baptism of Jesus, perhaps one of the most insightful views we have of John the Baptist is in this gospel.

While he may pointedly avoid referring to him, as John the Baptist, the fourth evangelist nonetheless respects John's God given purpose, highlighting his humble nature and presenting him as the ultimate witness to Christ. Here, John's role is that of witness, his purpose to testify to the light so that all might believe through him. The evangelist John describes him as being *'sent from God'* as a witness to testify to the light of the world, Jesus Christ:-

'He came for testimony, to testify to the light, so that all might believe through him. He was not the light, but came to testify to the light.' (John 1:7-8)

John does not deny John the Baptist's fulfillment of the scriptures and presents the baptism of Jesus as a testimony from John to underline his role as witness to the Messiah; a role which is as important as his role of forerunner and precursor.

It is also within the fourth gospel that John the Baptist refers to Jesus as the Lamb of God while acknowledging his pre-existence:-

'The next day he saw Jesus coming toward him and said, "Behold, the Lamb of God,* who takes away the sin of the world. He is the one of whom I said, 'A man is coming after me who ranks ahead of me because he existed before me'. (John 1:29-30),

From John's words it is clear that Jesus is born for the redemption of man and that all who come to him in true repentance will be granted forgiveness of sins and intercession at the throne of God. The sacrificial image of the Lamb of God is a theme that has been adopted throughout Christian history and derived from John's words.

Finally, it is in the gospel of John that we see Jesus himself describe John the Baptist as a *'burning and shining lamp'* (John 5:35) whose light people were once content to rejoice in.

Now, we have finally seen that John the Baptist has fulfilled all of the prophecies made by Angel Gabriel before his birth. He has indeed become great in the eyes of the Lord, avoiding strong drink and sometimes food; such was his commitment to fasting and prayer.

Filled with the Holy Spirit before he was born, he strengthened the presence of the spirit within him during his long time in the wilderness. It was undoubtedly that spirit the mesmerized the people who flocked to hear his preaching, confess their sins and receive his baptism of water on the banks of the River Jordan.

In doing all of this, John the Baptist did indeed turn the hearts of the people back to God, preaching repentance, reconciliation and the virtues of righteousness and finally preparing the people for the coming of the Messiah. In the baptism of Jesus, we reach the fulfillment of the prophets in the anointing of the Messiah by the spirit of Elijah manifested in John the Baptist. As the first witness to the Holy Trinity who has paved the way for the Holy Spirit, the ministry of John the Baptist is at an end.

The gamut of emotions of John the Baptist as he became the first witness of the Holy Trinity are not recorded and are impossible to comprehend in the heart of such a humble man. Filled with the Holy Spirit as he was and submissive to God's purpose for his life, however, John must have been aware that this was the culmination of his ministry.

While we can only guess at the complexity of emotions as he witnessed this portentous event, what we do know about John the Baptist is that he was a man of God, whose destiny was clearly defined by the Creator; a man born without original sin, who led a blameless life, obedient to God in all he did.

In his humility and submissiveness, John acknowledged that he must now step back to allow the light of Jesus to shine upon the world:-

"No one can receive anything except what has been given him from heaven. You yourselves can testify that I said [that] I am not the Messiah, but that I was sent before him. The one who has the bride is the bridegroom; the best man, who stands and listens for him, rejoices greatly at the bridegroom's voice. So this joy of mine has been made complete.

He must increase; I must decrease' (John 3:30).

From the time of his encounter with and baptism of Jesus, John's fulfillment of his own words began.

The Suffering of John the Baptist

As we have seen, John the Baptist's preaching was uncompromising and unrepentant in preparing the way for Jesus Christ. He responded to God's call on his life without question and his unorthodox appearance and ascetic lifestyle attracted not only the attention of a people yearning for the Messiah in the midst of a volatile political climate, but the authorities themselves.

Among them was Herod of Antipas, son of Herod the Great, an often ruthless ruler and tetrarch of Galilee. Herod was simultaneously in awe of and afraid of John the Baptist. The Jewish historian Josephus, writing in <u>Antiquities of the Jews,</u> describes the reaction of Herod of Antipas to the burgeoning popularity of this desert preacher:-

'When others too joined the crowds about him, because they were aroused to the highest degree by his sermons, Herod became alarmed. Eloquence that had so great an effect on mankind might lead to some form of sedition, for it looked as if they would be guided by John in everything that they did'.

Herod would not tolerate a potential threat to authority or a hint of sedition, as his father before him had not tolerated it.

Prophets of the Old Testament were often called to preach a message contradicting that of the rulers of the time and in return often suffered from their obedience to God.

For John the Baptist, the situation was to be no different. Josephus records the marriage of Herod of Antipas to Herodias, the wife of his brother, an act deemed unlawful according to the book of Leviticus.

John the Baptist was unflinching in his condemnation of Herod's behavior. While the tetrarch wanted to have John killed for his perceived insubordination, he refrained from doing so as he was afraid of the people's reactions:-

'Although Herod wanted to kill him, he feared the people, because they regarded him as a prophet'. (Matt 14: 5).

Ironically, Herod also reportedly protected John the Baptist from the wrath of his wife and stepdaughter, as he also considered him to be a *'holy and righteous man'. (Mark 6:20).*

Ultimately, the fate of John the Baptist was unavoidable. Herod later had him arrested and imprisoned for his outspoken opposition to Herod's marriage. John would have been aware that his condemnation of the marriage, while correct in the eyes of the law, would have been antagonistic to Herod. It is therefore likely that his arrest did not come as any surprise to him.

John the Baptist spent the remainder of his life incarcerated in the fortress of Machaerus lying on the shores of the Dead Sea, described by Josephus as a *'breathtaking palace'.*

That John was not immediately put to death is again attributed by some to Herod's fear of the crowd, and possibly his aforementioned recognition of John as a holy and righteous man.

John's ultimate demise came as a result of the manipulative scheming of Herod's wife Herodias and her daughter Salome, whose name is recorded in Josephus' Antiquities of the Jews, albeit not in the gospels. At a banquet given in celebration of his birthday, Herod's wife and stepdaughter contrived to end John's life.

After Herodias' daughter, Salome, pleased Herod by dancing for him and his guests, he promised her anything she wished for in return. After consulting with her mother, Herodias, who had nursed a long held grudge against John for his proclamations against her marriage to Herod, an agreement was reached between them.

Salome requested that John the Baptist's head be presented to her on a platter, a request which Herod the tetrarch was seemingly powerless to refuse.

John the Baptist was summarily executed and his head was given to Salome on a platter, who immediately presented it to her mother Herodias. *(Matt 14:8-11).* John's disciples later came and recovered his body, placing it in a tomb. Some doubt exists over the exact year of John's execution but it is estimated to have taken place around AD 28.

Such is John's pre-eminence, that with the exception of Jesus himself, his is the only birth and death that is recorded in the gospels.

Why was John the Baptist executed? The area where John preached and baptized was seen as a notorious area for revolutionaries and he was becoming increasingly popular. According to Josephus in his Antiquities of the Jews, the reasons for John's execution were clear:-

'Herod decided therefore that it would be much better to strike first and be rid of (John) before his work led to an uprising, than to wait for an upheaval, get involved in a difficult situation and see his mistake…'

The tetrarch was determined to prevent any revolution or uprising against him. Furthermore, the arrest and execution of John the Baptist was intended to put an end to the throngs of people flocking to the desert, an environment which may have provided a catalyst for sedition.

Despite his trust in God, imprisonment must have been difficult for John, particularly when facing the enmity of Herodias. He would have been aware that the purpose of his life was drawing to a close and scholars speculate on whether or not his faith was challenged. He may have been troubled by Jesus' enigmatic approach to his ministry while simultaneously facing his most challenging spiritual struggles since his time in the desert.

Jesus himself experienced unimaginable moments of the darkness of his soul in the garden of Gethsemane and on the cross. In his darkest moments, John the Baptist too may have felt abandoned by the God to whom he had committed his life. None of that is certain; what is known is that he was free to send messages as he dispatched his disciples to ask Jesus if he was the *'one who is to come, or should we expect someone else?' (Matt 11:2-3)* to which Jesus instructed his disciples to report details of his miracles and subtly confirm that he was indeed the Messiah:-.

Jesus said to them in reply, "Go and tell John what you hear and see: the blind regain their sight, the lame walk, lepers are cleansed, the deaf hear, the dead are raised, and the poor have the good news proclaimed to them. And blessed is the one who takes no offense at me." (Matthew 11:4-6)

Having met Jesus only once, at the time of his baptism, John would have sought confirmation that he had fulfilled God's purpose. This holy, sinless man was obedient to God's calling throughout his life, a life which paralleled that of Jesus himself.

John the Baptist and Jesus Christ: Parallels and Proclamation

While some scholars and historians often query whether or not John the Baptist was indeed the precursor to Christ and the prophet who he claimed to be, throughout Scripture we see evidence of the similar paths taken by both Jesus and his forerunner during their time on earth.

As a precursor and a forerunner to the Messiah it is perhaps unsurprising that the life of John the Baptist parallels that of the Son of God for whom he paves the way. Not only was John a relative of Jesus through his mother Elizabeth (thought by some scholars to be the cousin of Mary) but he was born only six months before him. Nowhere is this parallel life drawn as closely as in the opening chapter of Luke's gospel as John leaps in his mother's womb, full of the Holy Spirit as he recognizes the presence of the unborn Messiah.

Both births were announced by the Angel Gabriel, with their names chosen by God. As the Magnificat of Mary follows the announcement of her pregnancy, so the Canticle of Zechariah is revealed after John is born.

Little is known of either Jesus or John's early lives up until their public ministries. All that is mentioned of John is that the spirit of him grows strong, while Jesus is recorded as being found in his 'Father's temple' at around the age of twelve years old (*Luke 2:46*).

Jesus is not seen again until his baptism by John.

John the Baptist and Jesus were also subjected to persecution from the family of Herod, albeit at opposing times in their lives. The notorious Herod the Great persecuted Jesus' family while Jesus was an infant, forcing Joseph and Mary to flee Israel to protect the life of their infant Savior. John the Baptist, as we have seen, suffered the ultimate persecution from the descendant of Herod the Great, that of Herod of Antipas and his vengeful wife Herodias.

Jesus and John both endured times of trial in the desert. While it is believed that John the Baptist spent two decades in the desert wilderness, the temptation of Christ took place over forty days and nights immediately after his baptism, where he resisted all temptations placed before him by Satan. After his emergence from the desert, Jesus then began his ministry, like John the Baptist before him. Undoubtedly John suffered similar trials and temptations as he prepared for his ministry which are unrecorded.

The Holy Spirit also played a key role in the ministries of both John the Baptist and Jesus. John was clearly filled with the spirit before he was born and from that we can infer that the Spirit guided him during his desert sojourn, just as the Holy Spirit led Jesus too into the desert.

The words that began John the Baptist's ministry are identical to the words used by Jesus to begin his own, *'repent for the kingdom of God is near'*. Indeed, throughout his preaching, John pre-empted Jesus' own sermons, including his eschatological themes, his condemnation of sin and his reference to the wheat and the chaff, which can be found in the parables of Jesus.

As John referred to the religious authorities as 'vipers', so Jesus used those words himself and spoke of the seven Woes of the Pharisees (*Matt 23:1-39*). Both preached against self-righteousness and encouraged repentance among their followers. Jesus also echoed John's caution to the Jewish people not to rely on Abraham for their salvation, for this was a new covenant.

Both appealed not to the righteous but to sinners. The audiences of both John the Baptist and Jesus were predominantly society's rejects, numbering tax collectors, and prostitutes among them. The fact that women listened to both demonstrates the radical nature of their individual ministries in a society where women were subordinate to men in everything.

In preaching a new and radical message, John the Baptist laid the foundations for the new and radical preaching and the ministry of Jesus himself. His baptisms too were a precursor to Jesus, although he made clear that his was a baptism by water only. The baptism of the Holy Spirit could only come through the grace of Jesus Christ.

The opposition from the authorities endured by John the Baptist was apparent in his imprisonment and execution. The death and resurrection of Jesus was also pre-empted through John the Baptist here when we see the reaction of Herod of Antipas on hearing the stories of the miracles of Jesus. In his fear, Herod believed at first that it was '*John the Baptist, he has been raised from the dead*' *(Matthew 14:2).*

Perhaps too, John the Baptist's doubts and question of Jesus, as to whether or not he was the Messiah, is only a precursor of Jesus' own later torments on the cross when he cried out to a God who he momentarily feels has forsaken him *(Matt 27:45-46).*

While John's life parallels that of Jesus in so many ways, he is also his follower. John the Baptist was priest, prophet and servant in contrast to Jesus being priest prophet and king; he is the key to Jesus' ministry, key to the New Testament as a whole and viewed by many as the first Christian martyr.

These unavoidable parallels secure John's unassailable position in the grace and fulfillment of salvation history and of the life of Jesus. John is the precursor of Christ, the spirit of Elijah, bridging the gap between the New Testament and the Old to pave the way for Jesus Christ. In doing so he also becomes a boundary marker between the two ages.

Furthermore, while his time in the New Testament was necessarily brief, as the purpose of the gospels was to tell the story of Jesus, John the Baptist is referred to over ninety times throughout the Bible. Only Jesus, Peter and Paul are mentioned more than John, sure indication of his greatness.

Of course, it was not only the prophets and the angels who proclaimed the greatness of John the Baptist. Jesus himself, who was not heard praising his disciples – and in contrast often expressed frustration with them - recognized the greatness of John the Baptist in a remarkable passage found in Matthew's gospel.

Where John testified to the light of Jesus Christ in John's gospel, Jesus offered a testimony to his precursor, the man who paved the way for his ministry and who baptized him.

We have already seen how Jesus remarked in John's gospel on the people once being content to rejoice in John's light. Immediately after his Transfiguration, we have also seen Jesus' enigmatic reference to John as the spirit of Elijah.

In Matthew's gospel, Jesus proceeded to praise John the Baptist, while at the same time confirming his fulfillment of Scripture, referring to him as *'more than a prophet' (Matt 11:9)* and as the *'Elijah, the one who is to come' (Matt 11:14)*. In doing so, he also quoted directly from the book of Malachi. Jesus also drew a direct comparison between himself and John, commenting that while John was treated like a 'demon' for not eating and drinking, Jesus himself was regarded as a 'glutton and a drunkard'.

It is here too that we find the greatest accolade given to man by Jesus Christ, highlighted at the opening of this book that '… *among those born of women there has been none greater than John the Baptist;' (Matthew 11:11)*. Mysteriously, he then followed this claim with *'yet the least in the kingdom of heaven is greater than he'*.

In the midst of his praise and justification of John the Baptist, the words of Jesus may seem contradictory. Some scholars believe that Jesus was drawing the line between the old and the new with these words, with John representing the end of the law and the beginning of God's new blessing; that is, grace. From hereon, entering the kingdom of heaven will not be judged through works or adherence to the law. It will be through the grace of God given through faith in Jesus Christ

We must also look to St Jerome for a further explanation of Jesus words, taken from his <u>Homily 16</u>:-

'Now his meaning is: John is greater than all men, and if you want to know he is even an angel; nevertheless, he who is an angel on earth is the very least in the kingdom of heaven, that is, he is of a lesser rank than that angels. Moreover, he who is a minor in the kingdom of heaven, that is, an angel, is great than he who is greater than all men on earth'.

For Jesus, the Son of God and the fulfillment of all of the laws and the prophets, John the Baptist is pre-eminent among men as the prophet, forerunner and precursor of his ministry and life. His position in salvation history is confirmed; he provides a gateway to the gospels and is the boundary between the Old and New Testaments

Yet in doing so, John the Baptist had to finally step aside to allow prophecy to be fulfilled and for Jesus Christ to make the ultimate sacrifice and in doing so, 'take away the sin of the world'.

In being the precursor of Jesus, John the Baptist was also the disciple and follower of Jesus. As has been evident throughout, his life was one lived in total submission and trust to God, reflecting completely the words of Jesus in the gospel where he urged his followers to trust in God's *'kingdom and righteousness'* over material things and the distractions of the world. *(Matt 6:33)*.

It is John who demonstrated the ultimate denial in his early ministry in a rarely seen penance before God, surpassed only by Jesus himself and the Virgin Mary.

It is, finally, also John the Baptist who comes to mind when Jesus stated:

'Whoever loves father or mother more than me is not worthy of me' (Matthew 10:37).

Throughout his life and ministry, John the Baptist placed God's will above all earthly possessions and this detachment extended to friendship, family, his own emotions and ultimately his life. The continual practice of a mental and physical detachment manifested in him during his time in the desert enabled him to fulfill that purpose.

Ultimately, these seemingly parallel lives converged in the baptism of Jesus by John the Baptist, the only time that the forerunner and the Messiah actually met. Here John's ascendancy reached its apex and from that moment, as he understood it must be, he began to decrease.

He had testified to the light of the world and now the light of the world was upon mankind, John's own light must inevitably diminish.

The Veneration of John the Baptist

At the Council of Agde in 506, John the Baptist was deemed free from original sin and as such afforded a unique veneration in the history of Christianity, being honored each year on the day of his birth. Only the Virgin Mary and Jesus himself are given the same honor.

As a result, John the Baptist is celebrated on his birthday of 24th June (not the 25th due to the system of Roman counting) rather than on the anniversary of his beheading by Herod of Antipas, which is estimated to have been on 29th August. Some calendars mark both dates.

John the Baptist is revered by eastern and western traditions alike and has proved an inspiration to Catholic saints through the ages. Writing in '*A Treatise of Prayer*', St Catherine of Siena reveals how she called upon the example of John the Baptist as she responded to Satan's continual temptation of her soul:-

'Wretch that I am! John the Baptist never sinned and was sanctified in his mother's womb. And I have committed so many sins...'

The Blessed Anne Catherine Emmerich, who experienced many mystical visions during her life, once saw one of John the Baptist, free from sin before he was born. In a later vision she claimed to hear Jesus describe him as *'pure as an angel'*.

In addition, the author of <u>Meditations on the Life of Christ,</u> once thought to be St Bonaventure, described John the Baptist as a *'the chief and last of the patriarchs, . more than a prophet... the precursor of the Judge, ... Elijah and the law and the prophets cease with him'*.

For St Jerome, who venerated him above all saints, John the Baptist was the founder of Christian monasticism, represented in his lifelong self-denial and unswerving commitment to chastity and poverty and his obedience to God's will. The leather belt worn by John was also used as the basis of the monastic cingulum, an item worn by Christian monks. John the Baptist's ascetic approach to life could undoubtedly be seen as the infancy of monasticism in this hermit who wandered through the desert, preaching to the myriad crowds who would flock to hear his words.

St Augustine also pointed to John the Baptist as proof of the 'perfection' that a man can attain.

Through the centuries, the saint has been portrayed frequently in art; at times emaciated with long hair and a beard, at others portrayed as an archangel and a saint. Numerous churches are named after him, in addition to the largest Catholic University in the United States of America, that of St John's in Queens, New York State, which also carries the motto of 'Ecce Agnus' (Behold the Lamb) in its coat of arms.

Understandably, John the Baptist has also been the patron saint of an array of religious orders which practice asceticism and self-denial, such as the Augustinians, the Carmelites, the Carthusians and the Franciscans.

Through time, this has devolved to a wide range of professions from tailors to singers and to healing. In particular, he is seen as the healer of epilepsy, a legend which has its beginnings in the moments after his death. On seizing the decapitated head of John the Baptist from the platter on which it was presented, legend has it that Herodias collapsed in convulsions, foaming at the mouth and declaring that her soul would suffer eternal damnation.

While often being described as the first Christian martyr, the martyrdom of John the Baptist was, like his life, radically different to that of other saints.

Unlike the other Christian martyrs, he died without knowing the sacrifice that Jesus would make. In later years, that sacrifice would enable apostles like St Peter and St Paul to face their deaths stoically and with acceptance because they yearned to glorify Christ.

In facing his own death, John the Baptist lacked that reassurance. As the first witness to the Holy Trinity with an unflinching trust in God, however, his faith would have sustained him in his final moments.

Today many in the Catholic Church see him as second only to Mary as an intercessor before Christ.

Conclusion

St John the Baptist was the fulfillment of the prophets, the forerunner for Jesus, yet also his follower, the first Christian martyr and a man born without original sin, who lived a blameless life.

A humble soul, his call to holiness among all people and his emphasis on confession before baptism secures his pre-eminence in the Catholic faith. As an apocalyptic prophet, he surrendered his life to God, ministering for only two years after decades spent in the wilderness in a pursuit of God that is rarely seen today.

He was born to fulfill the prophecies, form a bridge between two eras of the law and the gospel and prepare a people for the Lord.

Blessed by the Holy Spirit from his conception, it seemed that all of Israel followed John into the desert for baptism and to hear his preaching. He knowingly risked his life to denounce Herod when he believed the tetrarch's marriage to be unlawful and ultimately paid for his words with his life.

He met Jesus only once but was the first witness to the Holy Trinity of God the Father, God the Son and God the Holy Spirit

The emphasis on the new era is in John's fulfillment of his purpose, which paved the way for Jesus Christ, reminding us all that we each have equal status in the Kingdom of God. Jesus himself paid tribute to John as being beyond a prophet; he is thus the greatest of humans, apart from the Virgin Mary.

He is wise, humble, Elijah revived and a man whose wisdom paralleled that of Jesus Christ himself.

St Paul refers to intention of the Holy Spirit as encouraging ministry within the church (*2 Cor 5:18*) and through his preaching, John personifies that. His powerful, God given insights influenced many to repent and reconcile themselves with God. Such was his presence, humility and devotion to God that he was at times mistaken for Elijah and Jesus himself.

That John the Baptist was a man of God is beyond doubt; he was the fulfillment of the prophecies of Isaiah, Malachi and Gabriel. As the precursor to Christ, his life was called to mirror that of his Savior, yet when the time came, he was subordinate to Jesus and submissive to God's will, gratefully decreasing so Jesus Christ could increase.

He represents a new beginning in the salvation history; the history of the Kingdom of God, which began with the baptism of Jesus by John the Baptist as the disciples made clear in the Book of Acts (*Acts 1:22*).

Through a life lived in self-denial, John the Baptist reminds Christians around the world that no-one is immune from judgment, while simultaneously urging confession and repentance to ensure reconciliation with God through Jesus. He encourages confession and avoidance of sin and the giving of alms. Above all, he understood the benefits of silence and reflection during prayers and devotions. In understanding true poverty, practicing total detachment, lacking pride and demonstrating only obedience, John epitomized the call of Jesus Christ for his followers to take up their cross and follow him, before the true meaning of his words were even understood.

While Jesus himself described John the Baptist as a burning and shining lamp, John understood he was born only to direct us to the light of the Savoir.

Expressing heartfelt gratitude for the sacrifice, suffering and dedication to God shown by John the Baptist, all Christians today can bask in the light of Jesus.

Indeed, today – and perhaps more than ever before - St John the Baptist remains the eternal *'voice crying out in the wilderness'*, a voice we should all flock to anew as we seek the grace and forgiveness of our Lord and savoir Lord Jesus Christ.

Prayers to Saint John the Baptist

Prayer to Saint John the Baptist

God, You raised up St. John the Baptist to prepare a perfect people for Christ. Fill Your people with the joy of possessing His grace, and direct the minds of all the faithful in the way of peace and salvation. Grant that, as St. John was martyred for truth and justice, so we may energetically profess our Faith in You, and lead others to the Way, the Truth, and Eternal Life. Amen.

Prayer to Saint John the Baptist II

O glorious Saint John the Baptist, greatest prophet among those born of woman, although thou wast sanctified in thy mother's womb and didst lead a most innocent life, nevertheless it was thy will to retire into the wilderness, there to devote thyself to the practice of austerity and penance; obtain for us of thy Lord the grace to be wholly detached, at least in our hearts, from earthly goods, and to practice Christian mortification with interior recollection and with the spirit of holy prayer.

Our Father, Hail Mary, Glory be

O most zealous Apostle, who, without working any miracle on others, but solely by the example of thy life of penance and the power of thy word, didst draw after thee the multitudes, in order to dispose them to receive the Messias worthily and to listen to His heavenly doctrine; grant that it may be given unto us, by means of thy example of a holy life and the exercise of every good work, to bring many souls to God, but above all those souls that are enveloped in the darkness of error and ignorance and are led astray by vice.

Our Father, Hail Mary, Glory be

O Martyr invincible, who, for the honor of God and the salvation of souls didst with firmness and constancy withstand the impiety of Herod even at the cost of thine own life, and didst rebuke him openly for his wicked and dissolute life; by thy prayers obtain for us a heart, brave and generous, in order that we may overcome all human respect and openly profess our faith in loyal obedience to the teachings of Jesus Christ, our divine Master.

Our Father, Hail Mary, Glory be

V. Pray for us, Saint John the Baptist
R. That we may be made worthy of the promises of Christ.

Let us pray.

O God, who hast made this day to be honorable in our eyes by the commemoration of blessed John the Baptist, grant unto Thy people the grace of spiritual joy, and direct the minds of all Thy faithful into the way of everlasting salvation. Through Christ our Lord. Amen.

Hymn to Saint John the Baptist

By Paul the Deacon

T hou, in thy childhood, to the desert caverns

Fleddest for refuge from the cities' turmoil,
Where the world's slander might not dim thy luster,
Lonely abiding.

Camel's hair raiment clothed thy saintly members;
Leathern the girdle which thy loins encircled;
Locusts and honey, with the fountain-water,
Daily sustained thee.

Oft in past ages, seers with hearts expectant
Sang the far-distant advent of the Daystar;
Thine was the glory, as the world's Redeemer
First to proclaim him.

Far as the wide world reacheth, born of woman,
Holier was there none than John the Baptist;
Meetly in water laving him who cleanseth
Man from pollution.

Praise to the Father, to the Sole-begotten,
And to the Spirit, equal power possessing,
One God whose glory, through the lapse of ages,
Ever resoundeth. Amen.

Made in the USA
Las Vegas, NV
10 February 2023

67281639R00030